# WALKING CONTAGIONS
## DALE BOOTON

polari                                    poetry

# Blood

rejected a dozen times by a jowly nurse who taps a pen against the filled in form says *you've had sex in the last 3 months lovey* yes oral only it didn't last long protected *that's still sex lovey* but I've been tested since then negative says *I'd love for you to help us it is really kind of you to want to do this but they have precautions for a reason* and I ask for the reason I ask why I cannot give what I have plenty of why a part of me won't sit mottled in a canister why a larger part of that part of me won't be taken cooled held for a time it is needed just as I sit and wait at home until I am needed

## Waiting

sat like strategically placed chess pieces
we eye up the competition
each pair of shaking legs a possible

or probable   before dropping like mallets
to our laps where fingers move
from knees to thighs to knees   tap

away like keys   silent ensemble of fear
we dare not speak or else
become too familial   too cautious

of the dry lips   watery eyes   skin paper
white like the printed result
that holds the secrets of our love

## When They Think of Gay

they think of anal   they think of a dick in someone's
arse   and then they wince
at their own imagination   they see animals
at play   sometimes kitted out in polished leather
harnesses   tied up the way good meat
is left hanging from the hook to soften before the
butchering   they think of back alleys
and toilet cubicles and parks after dark   they think of
limpness and campness and AIDS   unprotected
strangers in need of correction   *they can't help themselves
it is a part of their pathology*   all the sucking and the
wanking and the rimming and the fucking   *it is
all they know*   I'm telling you   when they think of gay
they think of anal   they don't think of love

## And I Could Preach of Heaven

of all the nameless angels I met in crowded bars
in nonamerequired hotel rooms   those quick-fix onenightstands
looking for something I couldn't quite explain
without first experiencing it   without
first holding it against myself
and feeling it entirely within myself   and I think
there was a time when I prayed for it
so hard   it seemed like a miracle
when it finally came in the shape of a man so divine
I thought he might be the one   that by his mere touch
he might save me   take me away   as if salvation
could be found at the fingertip-bridge of a stranger
my knees my church   his winged-eyes
singing a chorus the way yours had all those years ago

# Encounter

you wash yourself in my bathroom sink   hold your shaft
below the tap    feel the warmth of the water
as it snatches what parts of our time still lingers
disappears down the drain
the way you will from my little flat
and the next time we see each other your face will be a stubbed toe
beside your friend or your brother or your wife    and I
will have searched the mirror each day for purple islands
those atlas destinations spreading across the pages
of my sandy skin like the discoveries of
some other land    invaders of lucid dreams
and sweatsoldier marches to the bathroom
where I'll sit like The Thinker recounting the faces
of the men I have loved and have been loved by for a night

# Journal Fragments '82–'86

met a young guy down by Piccadilly station   told him
   he was beautiful   he was

mom called again today   couldn't put her off for a
   fifth time   said she's coming down because she wants to meet
   David   too late   it's been over for a week

there's a new cocktail at Dickie's   the drunken queen   delicious

had my 30th tonight   everyone was there   music   beer   cheers and
   David   he'd forgotten   of course   just came to
   collect the last of his things

Pete has found a great place in Soho   said it's to die for

Marty came by   Will's sick   really sick   he can't stand without
   fainting   has no idea what's causing it but it's bad

fuck   got called *daddy* last night   I'm officially dead   RIP me

Will's getting worse   mad fever and weird purple
   spots all over his body   no not spots   lesion things that grow

David came around   bled his heart out   we fucked
   and he said he'd call me in the week   we'll see if he does

it's AIDS   they don't really know what it is
   but it's a mean motherfucker   Will's got it which means
   Marty has it too

they're trying to cure it   so they say   like they actually care

Will's dead   Marty found him this morning

David came around   I've never seen him so pale   he has it
   too   told me to get checked but I feel fine   I'm not
   going to worry 'cause worrying makes it worse

mom's been calling all day   read about the *gay cancer* and
   now she's scared   she said she knew something bad would happen

Will's funeral today    Marty stayed last night    got shitfaced to cope

met a cute guy down by the gents    he was huge    nice ass too

Marty's dead    hung himself    I can't stop crying

everyone came to pay their respects    said he was
    too young to go

I don't want to leave the flat    how long have we got

sat in the clinic for an hour
    just sat
        I couldn't stand up and ask to be tested    felt dirty    scared

David came over    his new lover Sam has it    he's twenty-one    oh god

sat in the clinic again    it was too much    I don't want to know if    no

mom called    Jen's having a New Year's party and
    wants to know if I'll be able to make it

phones been ringing all day    more deaths    more diagnoses

sat in the clinic again with Pete    he held my hand    told me it will all be
    fine

I've got it

David called    mom called    David called again    I ignored them
    both    I don't want to talk to them    I don't want to
    talk to anyone

they have new information but still no cure

Pete's been diagnosed David's dead Sam's dying Rich is going crazy Thom
    has no idea where he is Phil is coughing up his blood Brian's funeral is
    tomorrow Ted's the day after and mine is to come

this has to stop

## If I Could Slay the Night

would I slit its dark throat and watch the stars
gush like mercury   scouring
the chords of its screams   the burning flesh of the sun
after a day that never seemed to end
the moon is so often a disco ball of sulphur
exploding like secrets   beauty

revealed   like the frenzied removing of
vest or socks or allcotton briefs
only ever cared for when notched into rain-stained marble
ours now scorched with paint welts   like the
purple filter over the ravishing lights
of the dancefloor

where we had our first kiss

## An Army of Lovers Must Not Die

i
no taxi will pick us up    it is as if
they know    his body
slumped in my arms    their hollow eyes gawping
at the clouded foam in the corners of his
mouth    his eyes climbing
to the back of his head in some effort
to hide this loss
of humility

ii
steps are steps    each one another rise from
the last    each one another
space closer

iii
your body is a classroom skeleton
draped in bin liners    loose
and unflattering    like that jumper you bought
too large but wouldn't
return

iv
in the bed you look like a puppet
trussed    each string
a lifeline    with some glances
I cannot tell what parts
of you
are you
and what parts are
them

v
*you shouldn't bring that in here
someone normal
might catch
it*

the coffee here is bland
and bitter

vi
I sit a while with your hand
in mine   the roughedsoftness of
your flesh   I bring it
to my lips

I have been warned
not to touch
you

# Bedside Pantomime

ACT ONE
sloshed water   foot in used bedpan
nurse in navy and white
smiles flatly as mother enters in leather gloves
shuffles slowly to the bed

*nurse*   your ma's here to see you

*patient (dazed)*   where

*nurse*   she's beside you

*mother (throat catching)*   I'm here   love

*nurse (clearing away)*   I'll give you some
   space   let me know if you
   need anything

door shuts   alone
hand clutching hand   flesh unbare
and bland   lips pursed
a snuffled laugh of awkwardness

*patient*   thank you   for coming

*mother*   what choice
   did I have   you're—
*patient*   how's dad

*mother*   he's fine   he's got to work
      otherwise I'm sure
         he'd be   here

elephant in the room
stomping silence into each corner
the iv drips   machines bleep
breath scarpers

*mother*   it's a nice room you've got

*patient (scoffs)*   yeah   think I'll stay here till I—

*mother (sternly)*   don't do   that

*patient*   I'm sorry   for that   for
        this   I guess I just got unlucky

*mother (distaste)*   unlucky   unlucky
            it isn't about luck   it was
            choice   your chose to be like—
            no   I need some air

INTERVAL
there is a family room down the hall
help yourself to tea   coffee   water
sometimes there are biscuits
please   take all the time you need

ACT TWO
nurse struggles to penetrate vein
hits binbag of flesh
instead   slight twinge
from patient   then coy smile

*nurse*   we'll have to do it again then
      won't we

dry chuckle from sore throat
success as door opens
mother returns   face pale   lips still pursed
hands still gloved

*patient*   just shooting up

nurse jeers   mother rolls her eyes
she never brought him up
like *this*   thinks if only he hadn't left
home   nurse leaves

*mother*   tell me this is some dream   some joke

*patient*   tell me mom   when did you last ask me
　how I am   who I am   when
　　did our flesh last touch

## Exposure, Part II

our bodies ache   on the streets where we rattle plastic cans
for change   we watch the flocks of low drooping eyes
scuttle by   like brambles in the north wind we
have become part of the scene   patient   hopeful   crying out
     but nothing happens

on the corner a preacher belts God's wrath on queers   I can hear
the snare tone of his voice as he echoes verse from the
tatty bible he clutches   there are few who stop and listen
to the dull rumour of God's war on fags   and wonder
     what are we doing here

across the street a man tugs the last cloud from his cigarette
lets his eyes wander up the pleated skirt of a
woman at the bus stop   she fans herself from the wet heat
her eyes hoping to catch a glimpse of that mottled red transport
     but nothing happens

the man catches a peek of the sun's irrevocable innocence
in her bronzed shoulders   then looks across at us
at our banner   chews his distaste as if it is milk freshly off
cocks his mouth as if ready to fire his first warning shot
     but nothing happens

leaves collect in the street   band together to line the kerb
like bouncers   we are the impatient sober waiting
for entry to watch our brothers and lovers dancing with
winged expressions of surrender   so this is where we end up
      is it that we are dying

Johno asks *Wilf should we call it a day*   stares down into his near-
empty can   at the piss-poor pennies dripped from unfeeling
hands   says *they don't give a shit about us   never have*
says *if they did they'd save us*   says *we don't have nobody but us*
      we turn back to our dying

a newspaper reads *Britain threatened by gay virus plague*   spits
our invasion of their land   shrieks the contagion of
our love   lauds the purification of our dying   smirks at
our ashes spilling like mountains disintegrating beneath their youth
      for love of God seems dying

tonight we will drag our ghosts home to our one already measuring
their hole in the ground   jokes *I probably shouldn't put on
any weight else I won't fit*   smiles like the crushed tablet taken
twice daily   says *when we're all gone   that's when they'll notice*
      but nothing happens

# I Hate It When I am Told

*it's a shame really   he's so nice isn't he*
as though you slabber salt into a wound that wasn't there
before your mouth opened   before you thought

if I can call it that   that your words
were a bandage to my ailment   a remedy to the sickness inside
that spills out in wades of blood and bruises

body collapsing on the pavement beside a chippy
late at night   light on   window filled with the pressed hands
and gawping eyes   voices not yet served

between fistfuls of chips   teeth hungry
for the last hit   the one that lets us know we'll be in the news
a few pages in saying *it's a shame really   he was nice*

## Wounded I Stand

as a testament of time   if they will allow my testament
a page in that grand book they call *history*   as if
history is anything but wounded

I am one voice in a sea of one million billion trillion voices
shouting out   the thrashing of our tongues spitting
shards from our throats that are wounded

the lawman-thugman comes with his truncheon raised   spits
teargas from his mouth   screams the law of freedom that
cuts the flesh to jail time   locks away the wounded

I have clawed my way from bar to bar   found only headstones
where stalls should be   found only ashes where
dancers discovered they were wounded

our pleads of *help us  we are dying*   bouncing off the wells
that we had come to wish at   tossing pennies to the
lonely water that could not cure the wounded

among the horns and rev of traffic   I hear the salt crusted shouts of
your disgust flung from your car window at speed   trying to rip
the colours from our flag   as if our Pride could be wounded

from beginning to end   they have kept us wounded
our names   our words   our memories   our love are all wounded

# I Wonder How Many I Have Killed with My Love

I sip my rum punch and try to remember
the names of those I had asked for   the faces
of those I didn't   they blur before me
like New York frost on a windscreen

how sweet their voices had tasted   the soft-shoe
shuffle of their tongue on the dancefloor
the quick-step press of their ass
in the bathroom and on the stairs

leading out to the night's loud furnace
of cabs and clubs and kisses
in subway cars and coveted corners
where the moon's shadow obscured all

but the ravishing of flesh in the mouth
a chorus of eyes like sea dwellers
awaiting that tidal wave of
life to flood out over the pavement

or down a throat   or to be buried
between the squat cheeks of a twink
moaning love yous to a stranger   not unfriendly
not uncaring   rough   not too rough

# A Gift

all day the rain has pleaded for my
attention   danced its naked
self like a go-go down the stage of my
window   and I've hoped
that the sun wouldn't show its face
wouldn't rise to greet
it with its warm tongue   so
bent on drinking it up   as I sit
so intent on watching it in all its
wet beauty   because I know that as
I watch it *you* will be
somewhere watching it
too   your eyes flexed on the sky
as it pours

## Gay Men are Old at Thirty

because we tell ourselves that   in our best sex ed teacher
voice *when a man loves a woman   they get married
have a family*   and we   so many of us
throughout the years   lonely and afraid to love

sat apart from the rosy smile   the peony eyes
the hands as roots stretching out to meet
ground that cannot be found   as though the heart is a fruit
that never ripens enough to eat

i am so hungry   my body malnourished and frail
like a vacuum-packed mattresses   i long
to spring from my plastic fitting   stare in the mirror
in my best therapist voice *and how does that make you feel*

[ ]   and here i am mixing too much metaphor and imagery
like a tent or a sleeping bag i pack away
too much of myself into myself
gawk at the busstop body   the frame already

begun to rust   the eyes like shattered safetyglass
on the verge of collapse
lips as tickets
but the date keeps getting pushed back

## Another Season in Hell

once   if my memory serves me well   my life was a
banquet where every heart revealed itself
beneath the gentle cooing of the moon's breath   not
1km apart behind the green dot on the phone screen
typing *hey wuu2   tp or bttm?   how big?   fun?*

scrolling through nameless faces and headless torsos
and pictureless profiles where taglines are sizes
too small for words beyond *chillin* and *k*
behind *2 cool 4 skool* attitudes of men sickly certain
of their prominent dominance   *bow down in awe*

you are not God's gift to gaykind!
you are not the be all and end all of homo-life

and yet   shrouded in a private moonlight   I tap my way
to caress the filtered farce of our love   red-faced and
cradled   breathing the flustered husk of our passion
two times over   sailing in the sea-salt sweat
of sex done well   our love a mere *I accom* away

and I may message *hi*   my delusion deep-set   the way
a child believes fairy tales true   I believe that
if I hit the tap button daily you might acknowledge
me   and I won't have to rely on my pillow
being the dingy that keeps me afloat through till morning

## U = U

the daffodils are dancing like the young men
I have often seen in clubs   lost
to the sound of the ardent air   their arms
like stems that have been holding the weight
of themselves in their hands
for too long

I think I was this way too when I first said it
out loud to another person   as if
the secret was the root of a weed I needed to tear up
as if replacing it with only the prettiest
flowers might release me
from the shame

from the idea that my body has been invaded
that my cells play house to a loaded
pollen fired from the stamen that never
stayed   he left more than his promise of a night
of love   that my future nights
might be loveless

because the medicine isn't just the daily
pill popping   it's the tending of my kempt garden
with the efforts I might call ripe adoration
it's the knowing that the bud of
the poisoned petals I hold within me
won't ever bloom

# Epilogue

I am wondering / if / after I walk into light / I will be met by the men / who have come / and gone / like cheap shoes worn away / by the soles of others / how they loved and / lost / themselves / crossing the roads to unknown / apartments / bathroom stalls / canal edges / where pleasure / was a temptation / too good to miss / o how they are missed / and are / missing / their shoes their trousers their jockstrap / left / unbulged on the floor / of the bedroom or livingroom / of a love / without a name / o how they kissed and wanked and sucked and rimmed and fucked / 69'd into paradise / by a motormouthed profile / headless / shot of torso / tainted bronze steel / coloured beige or brown or night / or that colour / of cum / what is it? / glossy white? / a sort of spermy light / like ending / as I began / the lucky / one

# Notes

**'Blood'** is after Andrew McMillan's poem 'Blood' and takes the line 'mottled in a canister' from that poem. It is about the three-month deferral policy on gay/bi men who want to donate blood and was published by Untitled: Voices.

**'And I Could Preach of Heaven'** was published by Queerlings.

**'Journal Fragments '82–'86'** was a commended poem in the Verve Poetry Press 2020 competition and was published in the *We've Done Nothing Wrong. We've Got Nothing to Hide Diversity* anthology.

**'An Army of Lovers Must Not Die'** is dedicated to Larry Kramer and takes its title from the unfinished play he was working on before his death.

**'Exposure, Part II'** won second prize in the August Challenge #1: Re-mixing History, Fiction and the Unexpected and was published by The Poetry Society. The final line of each stanza is taken directly from the original poem by Owen.

**'Wounded I Stand'** is after خڅمستان (wounded-i-stan) by Suhrab Sirat. It was published by The Adriatic.

**'Another Season in Hell'** is after Arthur Rimbaud's 'A Season in Hell' and takes its first two lines from that poem: 'once, if my memory serves me well, my life was a banquet where every heart revealed itself'.

**'Epilogue'** takes a portion of its first line – 'I am wondering / if / after I walk into light / I will be met by' from Joelle Taylor's poem 'Got a Light, Jack?'.